Who Was
Julia Child?

Who Was
Julia Child?

by Geoff Edgers and Carlene Hempel

illustrated by Dede Putra

Penguin Workshop

To Bobi, for poppy-seed cookies, blintzes,
and that outrageous lasagna—GE

To my mother and father, both wonderful cooks,
who loved to watch Julia Child on Channel 2
with me when I was a girl—CH

PENGUIN WORKSHOP
An Imprint of Penguin Random House LLC, New York

Visit us online at www.penguinrandomhouse.com.

Library of Congress Control Number: 2015953984

ISBN 9780448482972   10 9 8 7 6 5 4

Contents

Who Was
Julia Child?

One night in 1962, people watching Channel 2 in Boston saw something unexpected. There, standing over a frying pan, was a woman tall enough to play professional basketball. She wore an apron and spoke in a fluttering, high-pitched voice. She was excited.

Julia Child was cooking an omelet.

That's a fancy way of making scrambled eggs that are served folded in half.

The show's producers were not expecting Julia to be a big hit. Back then, the most popular shows were westerns, cartoons, and comedies. There certainly weren't many people cooking on television.

And Americans were not doing much cooking

in general. In the early 1960s, the economy was booming. New cars, new stereos, and new appliances were introduced. Women were beginning to work hard at building their careers. TV dinners, frozen in metal trays and warmed in the oven, were popular. The idea of spending time cooking a complicated meal seemed old-fashioned!

Julia Child wanted to change that. She cooked her omelet for less than one minute in a sizzling-hot buttery pan on live television. And one minute was all it took for viewers to fall in love with her. By the next morning, they were calling the TV station and writing letters. They wanted to see more of Julia's cooking. And they got their wish.

Julia began taping her own half-hour cooking show called *The French Chef.* At first it was shown only in the Boston area. But eventually it could be seen on televisions across the country.

She showed people that cooking could be fun and rewarding and special. She reminded them that meals could be crafted with great care and love.

Flipping her omelet that day, Julia had no way of knowing that she would become so famous. Her cookbook would eventually sell millions of copies. Julia would be on the cover of magazines and a guest at the White House. Her kitchen would be put on display at one of the most important museums in the United States.

Through it all, Julia Child never forgot why she put on her apron. She loved cooking and sharing a great meal with friends. Julia turned housewives into chefs. She turned chefs into TV stars.

At the end of each television show, she would wave to her audience, taste a forkful of what she had just prepared, and utter two French words she made famous: *Bon appétit!* (say: bun appa-TEE).

That's French for "good appetite." Julia wanted everyone to eat well and to enjoy their meals with friends and family. She brought her hearty appetite for life to everything she did.

Chapter 1
Growing Up in California

John McWilliams met Julia Carolyn Weston at the Chicago World's Fair in 1903. Julia had gone to Smith College and came from a wealthy family that owned a paper company. Though her first name was Julia, everybody called her Caro, short for her middle name, Carolyn.

The young couple got married and moved to Pasadena, California. John took over his family's banking business. Their first child, Julia, was born on August 15, 1912.

As a child, Julia was full of energy and a fearless sense of adventure. On her tricycle, she roamed the neighborhood without telling anybody where she was going. As Julia got older, she rode her bike everywhere. She rode so fast people called her a daredevil.

She also loved jokes and pranks, even if they sometimes went too far.

Once, she figured out a way to get around one of the family's big rules: No dogs on their summer vacation at a beach house.

Julia's father thought the dog would make a mess. But Julia sneaked her dog, Eric the Red, into a laundry basket. She hid the basket in the car. By the time anybody noticed, it was too late to turn back. Eric the Red was on his way to the beach!

Julia's parents loved how clever and mischievous she was. They did whatever they could to make sure she was happy. As a result, she grew into a content and confident girl.

Julia did not have to worry about much. Her wealthy family lived in a big house. Julia had a wall of stuffed animals. The family had a maid and nurse who lived with them. They took care of Julia and her younger brother and sister, John and Dort. Dort's real name was Dorothy, but Julia called her "Dort the Wort."

From the start, Julia stood out. She was always taller than the other kids. In class pictures, the school photographer always told Julia to stand in the back row. That way she wouldn't block the other children.

Her height also helped her to be a great athlete. In softball, she impressed everyone by throwing the ball as hard as a boy. In basketball, she was the tallest girl on the team and made the most baskets.

Growing up under the warm California sun also allowed Julia to fill her days with swimming and climbing sand dunes all year round.

When they were old enough, all the McWilliams children were sent to private high schools and lived away from home. At fifteen, Julia went to the Katherine Branson School.

KATHERINE BRANSON SCHOOL

The all-girls school was very strict. Students wore uniforms and went to church every Sunday. Julia struggled in class. She found it hard to learn French, and she barely passed her other classes. But she loved making friends and learning new things. Although her grades weren't the best, Julia joined many school activities.

She was captain of the basketball team and president of the school's student council and hiking club. She was also a member of the Fantastics, the drama group. She always wanted to play a queen or a princess, but that didn't happen. "I was usually cast as a fish or something," she once said, "never as the beautiful princess." And she was often asked to perform the men's roles because of her height.

By the time Julia graduated in 1930, everybody
knew her. She was very popular. She was even
awarded the school cup by Ms. Katherine Branson
herself. That's an honor given to one senior
who best demonstrated the spirit of the school.

At graduation Ms. Branson had said that Julia was
a "practical, wholesome type of girl with superior
intelligence." She meant that Julia was special and
it was only a matter of time before everyone else
knew it.

Chapter 2
An Independent Life

SMITH COLLEGE

Julia was accepted into Smith College in Massachusetts, the same school her mother had gone to. When she arrived at Smith, Julia was asked to write down what sort of job she hoped to have one day. "No occupation," she answered.

"Marriage preferable." She decided to major in history.

Julia's classmates were smart and worked hard. Julia didn't study much. At one point, she had all Cs and even worried about failing out of college.

In 1934, Julia graduated from Smith. She still had no plans for a career, but her school advisors weren't worried. One of them noted in a report that Julia's family was wealthy. "She will not need a job."

Her advisor had been right. After graduation, Julia returned home to Pasadena. Aimless, she roamed the house reading books and playing piano.

She went to the movies. In 1935, Julia's sister Dorothy was accepted into Bennington College in Vermont. Julia had nothing to do at the end of that summer, so she and Caro drove Dort back to school on the East Coast.

That gave Caro an idea. She would have Julia stay with her Aunt Theodora in Massachusetts and go to school to become a secretary. Julia was not at all interested, but she had nothing else to do. She lasted only a month.

Around the same time, she was contacted by the career office at Smith. Would she like to work for the W. & J. Sloane furniture company in New York City? They needed someone to set up photography shoots, write press releases, and do odd jobs. The pay was only eighteen dollars a week—much less than what she would need to live in New York—but Julia took it.

She was twenty-three, and she loved city life. She went to operas, plays, and nightclubs with friends. She barely cooked. Instead, she ate at cheap restaurants to save money. Julia wanted a glamorous life. And she dreamed of becoming a writer for a famous magazine, so she sent articles to *The New Yorker* and applied to *Time* magazine and *Newsweek*. But nobody hired her.

As much as Julia loved New York, she eventually thought her job was boring, and she longed for an adventure. But what would that adventure be? In the spring of 1937, Julia quit her job and went back home to California.

She was happier there, but not for long. Her mother became sick with kidney disease. Caro was only sixty when she died that summer.

Julia's father was crushed. The family had a cook and butler who took care of him, but John McWilliams was too sad to live without his family. So, for the next five years, Julia stayed home to keep him company.

Her father wanted Julia to get married and have children. And he had just the right guy in mind for her. Harrison Chandler, the wealthy son of the owner of the *Los Angeles Times*, liked Julia. In 1940 he proposed.

HARRISON CHANDLER

John pressured Julia to accept. But she wanted to love the man she would marry. And she didn't love Harrison. She said no. Then something unexpected happened that changed life for Julia and the entire country.

On December 7, 1941, the Japanese bombed
Pearl Harbor, a port in Hawaii.

The United States was now at war. Julia, like many Americans, wanted to do something to help.

WORLD WAR II

WORLD WAR II BEGAN IN 1939 WHEN GERMANY INVADED POLAND AND MADE PLANS TO ATTACK FRANCE. GERMANY, ALONG WITH JAPAN AND ITALY, BECAME KNOWN AS THE AXIS POWERS. THE AXIS NATIONS WERE FIGHTING AGAINST THE ALLIED POWERS FOR CONTROL OF EUROPE AND ASIA.

THE UNITED STATES JOINED THE WAR ON THE SIDE OF THE ALLIES, WHICH INCLUDED THE SOVIET UNION, CHINA, AND THE UNITED KINGDOM, IN 1941, AFTER THE BOMBING OF PEARL HARBOR, HAWAII.

THE WAR ENDED IN 1945 AFTER THE ALLIES INVADED GERMANY AND THEN DROPPED ATOMIC BOMBS ON HIROSHIMA AND NAGASAKI, TWO CITIES IN JAPAN.

MORE THAN SIXTY MILLION PEOPLE DIED DURING WORLD WAR II—MORE THAN DURING ANY OTHER WAR.

In 1942, Julia moved to Washington, DC, and applied to both the army and the navy. Amazingly, she was rejected. "I was too long," is how she explained it. At six feet two inches, the army and navy both felt that Julia was too tall! But Julia wasn't about to go back to Pasadena.

Julia heard about the Office of Strategic Services, one of the most top secret agencies in the US government. It was hiring only the smartest people. Some OSS workers went undercover to get information for the United States. They were spies! It sounded exciting to Julia, so she applied. No one at the OSS cared how tall she was, and she got the job.

At first, Julia simply filed papers. Her boss, though, could tell Julia was very smart. It didn't take long for Julia to get a promotion. She was asked to work in the office of the man in charge of the OSS, General William J. Donovan.

THE OSS

PRESIDENT
FRANKLIN ROOSEVELT

PRESIDENT FRANKLIN ROOSEVELT CREATED THE OFFICE OF STRATEGIC SERVICES (THE OSS) IN 1942 TO GATHER SECRET INFORMATION DURING WORLD WAR II. OSS WORKERS SPIED ON OTHER COUNTRIES, SNEAKED INTO ENEMY TERRITORY, AND INVENTED NEW WEAPONS. THESE INVENTIONS INCLUDED A GRENADE DISGUISED AS A BAG OF FLOUR. GENERAL WILLIAM J. DONOVAN WAS IN CHARGE OF THE OSS. HE WAS CALLED "THE FATHER OF AMERICAN INTELLIGENCE."

AFTER WORLD WAR II ENDED, THE GOVERNMENT CLOSED THE OSS. BUT IN 1947, A NEW INTELLIGENCE AGENCY WAS CREATED TO TAKE ITS PLACE. CALLED THE CENTRAL INTELLIGENCE AGENCY, OR CIA, ITS GOAL IS TO GATHER AND ANALYZE INFORMATION AS WELL AS TO CARRY OUT TOP SECRET MISSIONS.

As the war continued, General Donovan asked Julia if she would be willing to travel overseas. Of course she would! Julia was thrilled to get a chance for a real adventure. Early in 1944, Julia boarded the SS *Mariposa* for a journey that would take more than a month at sea. She was headed to Sri Lanka, an island on the other side of the world, in the Indian Ocean.

Julia read top secret reports and organized the information on nearly ten thousand index cards. She worked hard on this serious mission.

The OSS gave Julia a chance to see different parts of the world. She traveled from Sri Lanka to China. For the first time in her life, she tried new and exciting foods. She met people from other countries and other cultures. And it was while working for the OSS that Julia met the man who would change her life.

Chapter 3
Julia and Paul

In 1944, Julia's friends introduced her to Paul Child. Paul was also working for the OSS in Sri Lanka. At first, Julia wasn't impressed. "I thought, not at all nice looking," she wrote in her diary. Paul had almost

PAUL CHILD

no hair, and he was ten years older. He was also about five inches shorter than Julia.

Paul wasn't much interested in Julia, either. He
thought Julia was too young to be his girlfriend.
But Paul and Julia began to spend a lot of time
together. They explored ancient temples on the
island. They watched elephants walking in the
mountains. They had picnics. Their feelings for
each other started to grow stronger.

In early 1945, the OSS sent Paul to work in Kunming, China. Paul wrote letters to Julia, telling her how much he missed her. Then, in March 1945, Julia was reassigned to Kunming, too! She was thrilled.

In China, the army food served on their base was horrible. Canned tomatoes, boiled potatoes, even stewed water buffalo. Julia and Paul refused to eat it and began to visit local restaurants together. The food in Kunming restaurants was amazing! Julia and Paul ordered plates of rice noodles, chicken, and duck.

Julia couldn't believe how much Paul knew about food. He had spent years traveling for his job. He taught Julia that trying new foods was an exciting way to learn about new cultures. He also taught her that eating could be its own adventure.

Paul loved Julia's willingness to eat anything on her plate. She was always willing to try something new. She was quickly becoming the woman of his dreams.

When the war ended in 1945, Julia was sent back to Washington, DC. The OSS sent Paul to Peking,

another city in China, for a few months. That's when he finally put his feelings for Julia in a letter.

"Why aren't you here, holding my hand and making plans for food and fun!" he wrote to her.

Julia wrote back the same day she received his letter. She told Paul that she loved him. They promised to never, ever be apart again.

Chapter 4
Moving to Paris

Julia returned to the United States in the fall of 1945. Paul followed early in 1946. After ten months apart, Julia and Paul decided to take a vacation and visit family and friends. They started in California. Julia introduced Paul to her father. John McWilliams wasn't thrilled. He still wanted Julia to marry Harrison Chandler! That didn't matter to Paul and Julia. They were in love.

They started driving east in Julia's car. After a month, they reached the other end of the country: Maine. That's where Paul's brother Charlie had a summer cabin. Charlie and his family loved meeting Julia.

Julia and Paul made plans to get married on September 1, 1946, at the home of some friends in New Jersey. Julia's father flew in from California. Dort drove from New York City. John came from

Massachusetts. And Charlie's family also made their way to New Jersey.

The day before the wedding, a truck lost control and slammed into Paul and Julia's car. They were rushed to a local hospital. Julia had broken glass removed from her arm. Paul needed a cane to walk. But Julia wouldn't consider canceling the wedding.

The next day, Julia and Paul walked together through their friends' beautiful garden. It was a simple wedding with no band or bridesmaids. About twenty-five people came. Julia wore a brown-and-white polka-dot dress. She also had a big bandage to cover the stitches on her face. But Julia didn't mind! She was so happy. She was no longer Julia McWilliams. Julia was thirty-four years old, and she was now Julia Child.

Paul got a new job working at the State Department of the US government. So the young couple moved to Washington, DC. Julia did not want to be a secretary ever again. Instead, she decided she would do her best to be a housewife.

She wanted to decorate their new home and to learn how to cook.

This wasn't easy for Julia. Many children grow up learning how to cook from their parents. They bake cookies or brownies at home. They learn how to use the stove and how to follow a recipe. Julia had never experienced any of that. The McWilliams family had had a cook. As a child Julia was never even allowed in the kitchen!

Julia read lots of cooking magazines. But she found them difficult to follow. She had a lot of enthusiasm but very few real skills in the kitchen.

Paul didn't mind. He loved having Julia as his wife, and that's all that mattered to him.

When the US government created a new department called the United States Information Service, their goal was to teach people in other countries about Americans through culture and art. They needed someone to organize art exhibitions. In 1948, the agency asked Paul if he would move to France to take over the project. The offer seemed perfect. Paul loved Paris. He had lived there when he was younger. And Julia was looking for another adventure. She also looked forward to trying French food.

They got on a boat in late October and sailed to France. When they arrived, they drove through the French countryside to Paris. Along the way they stopped in a small town for lunch. It was November 3, 1948. Julia would always remember that date. It is when she and Paul had lunch at a restaurant called La Couronne (say: la COOR-an).

Paul spoke French, so he ordered the food.
First, oysters. Delicious. Next came the main
course, Sole Meunière (say:
mun-YER). The chef
cooked the fish very
simply in a pan with
lots of butter. Then he

sprinkled parsley and lemon juice over the dish.

"The waiter carefully placed the platter in front

of us, stepped back, and said: 'Bon appétit!'" (say: bun appa-TEE). The waiter was wishing them a "good appetite" and hoping they would enjoy their meal. Julia closed her eyes as the smell rose from the pan. She ate each forkful slowly. "It was the most exciting meal of my life," she later wrote.

For days, Julia ordered Sole Meunière everywhere she and Paul went. Then she started trying all kinds of new and exciting food. Julia fell in love with French food and Parisian culture.

She wandered through the city's charming streets. She spent time in cafés drinking coffee. She quickly made friends and went to lots of parties with Paul. She found an apartment for the two of them with an amazing view of the city.

Julia stayed busy taking a class on hat making and also playing cards with other housewives.

But these hobbies bored her. Julia was almost forty. She missed having her own career.

She signed up for French classes so that she could speak the language. Then a friend made a suggestion. Didn't Julia love French food? Why didn't she take the time to learn to cook?

If you were going to take cooking classes in Paris in the 1940s, there was only one place to go: Le Cordon Bleu (Say: luh cord-on BLUH). On October 6, 1949, Julia showed up for her first class at the world-famous cooking school.

LE CORDON BLEU

A FRENCH JOURNALIST NAMED MARTHE DISTEL WANTED TO OFFER REGULAR PEOPLE A CHANCE TO TAKE COOKING LESSONS WITH A PROFESSIONAL CHEF. PEOPLE LIKED THE LESSONS SO MUCH THAT DISTEL FOUNDED A SCHOOL TO TEACH PEOPLE HOW TO COOK. IT OPENED IN 1895.

SHE CALLED THE SCHOOL LE CORDON BLEU (THE BLUE RIBBON). IN FRANCE, CORDON BLEUS WERE THE BLUE RIBBONS GIVEN OUT TO THE HIGHEST-RANKING KNIGHTS CENTURIES EARLIER.

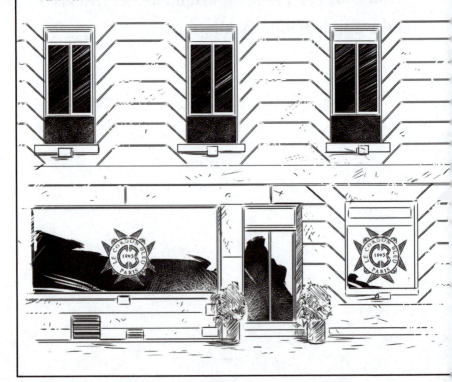

LE CORDON BLEU WOULD TEACH PEOPLE TO AIM FOR THE SAME EXCELLENCE IN THE KITCHEN.

MARTHE DISTEL

MOST OF THE SCHOOL'S STUDENTS WERE ORIGINALLY WEALTHY HOUSE-WIVES. IN FRANCE, ONLY MEN HAD BEEN ALLOWED TO LEARN TO COOK BY STUDYING IN THE KITCHENS OF FRENCH RESTAURANTS. LE CORDON BLEU GAVE WOMEN A CHANCE TO LEARN FROM PROFESSIONAL CHEFS IN A CLASSROOM, RATHER THAN IN A RESTAURANT.

MORE THAN ONE HUNDRED YEARS LATER, LE CORDON BLEU HAS ADDED SCHOOLS AROUND THE WORLD. TODAY, THERE ARE MORE THAN FORTY SCHOOLS AND MORE THAN TWENTY THOUSAND CORDON BLEU STUDENTS ON FIVE CONTINENTS.

Chapter 5
Cooking Class

Julia's first day at the famous Le Cordon Bleu did not go well. She was in a class for beginners. Her classmates were two women who couldn't even boil an egg in water! Julia was ready for something more challenging.

She marched down the hall to meet with Madame Brassart, the school's director.

Madame Brassart insisted that Julia should stay in the beginners class. She was certain that most Americans couldn't cook at all.

Julia refused so forcefully Madame Brassart had no choice. She moved Julia to a class for professional cooks.

The next morning, Julia found that the students in her new class were all men. Many of

them had served in World War II as army cooks.
They were not interested in complicated recipes.
They just wanted to improve their cooking skills
so they could open their own small restaurants.

Julia wasn't at all nervous about being the only woman in a class of ex-soldiers. She was used to standing out. She tied on her apron and took her

CHEF MAX BUGNARD

place at the counter.
Her teacher was Chef Max Bugnard. He had been cooking in French restaurants for more than sixty years. Chef Bugnard had round glasses and a thick mustache. He didn't treat Julia like an outsider.
Very quickly, he saw how excited she was to learn French cooking. He would be her guide.

To become a great chef, Julia would have to devote all her time to cooking. So she did.

Her classes started early every morning. After class, Julia went straight to the local food market. She bought the ingredients she needed to cook what had been taught in class that morning. She headed back home to practice.

And Julia was determined to practice until she got her recipes just right. She wrote down notes as she cooked. She kept track of her successes and the meals that didn't turn out well. That way, she would not repeat her mistakes.

 Julia learned to follow recipes. It wasn't enough to sprinkle a little of this and a little of that into the pot. Ingredients needed to be measured exactly.

Julia spent hours every day cooking. Paul began to notice.

"Julie's cookery is actually improving," he wrote his brother. "I didn't quite believe it would, between us, but it really is."

After more than a year at Le Cordon Bleu, Julia was ready to graduate. Chef Bugnard spoke to Madame Brassart, who agreed to schedule Julia's final exam.

It was April of 1951, and Julia had been studying hard for months. She knew how to make all sorts of difficult recipes. But the exam caught her by surprise. Julia was asked to write down the ingredients to a recipe she had never heard of!

Julia panicked and began to make up a list of ingredients. When the results were announced, Julia couldn't believe it. She had failed her final exam.

Later that year, Julia retook the exam and passed. She had finally graduated. But she never forgot failing her first exam at Le Cordon Bleu.

Chapter 6
A Cookbook Like No Other

Julia was angry at herself for having to take
the exam twice at Le Cordon Bleu, but she
wasn't the type of person to stay angry for long.

She continued to go to fun parties with Paul and enjoy her time in Paris. There was always a chance she'd discover a new recipe or get to meet another chef.

One warm June night in 1951, Julia went to a fancy party in Paris with Paul. She met a lot of new people.

One of them was Simone Beck Fischbacher. Simone instantly liked Julia, and when she heard about Julia's work at the cooking school, she told her all about a club for women who liked to cook French food. Julia was excited and happy to join. Every other Tuesday, she, Simone, and the others would cook and eat lunch together at each other's houses. They would share old recipes and learn new ones. Julia also grew closer to Simone, whose best friends called her Simca.

Simca and Julia had a lot in common. They both had taken classes at Le Cordon Bleu. They both loved to cook French food more than anything else in the world. And they both had kitchens stocked with every kind of cooking tool a professional chef would use.

SIMONE BECK
FISCHBACHER

Simca soon had an idea—a big one. She asked Julia if she would be interested in starting a cooking school with her. They could use Julia's amazing kitchen and ask Simca's friend Louisette Bertholle to help out.

Within seven months, the three women
opened their school. They called it L'Ecole des
Trois Gourmandes. In English, that means "the
School of the Three Hearty Eaters." They would
only teach American students who wanted to
cook French food, and they would only charge
five dollars for a lesson and lunch. In late 1952,

they held their first four-hour class for three
American women.

"I've finally found a real and satisfying
profession which will keep me busy well into
the year 2000," Julia wrote to her pen pal, Avis
DeVoto.

Even before they had opened the School of the Three Hearty Eaters, Simca and Louisette had been working on a French cookbook. They wanted to publish something for American housewives. Since Julia was American and a great cook, she seemed like the perfect partner. Julia was delighted to help.

There were about six hundred different dishes to make in the pile of recipes Simca and Louisette handed to Julia. First, Julia started cooking the recipes one by one. But Julia didn't make each recipe just once. She created each one over and over,

sometimes working for up to fourteen hours
a day in her kitchen. Simca and Louisette had
been using French measurements. But American
measurements are very different. A cup of flour is
measured in grams in France, not in ounces. Julia
also thought their instructions were incomplete.

If a recipe said to put "a pinch" of salt into
a soup, that was not good enough for Julia.

She wanted the recipes to be exact. This was going to be a book for anyone who wanted to cook French food. It was not for professional chefs. So, Julia figured out what a "pinch" actually was when measured, and wrote that into the recipe.

Julia didn't mind the work. She told her pen pal Avis that she had come to believe they were writing a "classic"—a book that would live on forever. She also started to think of certain recipes she was creating as "TOP SECRET," a message she always wrote to Avis in all capital letters.

Many of the original recipes were from Simca and Louisette's families. They had been passed down from grandmothers to mothers. So it is not surprising that Julia's two partners didn't want her to change the recipes in any way. The three friends began to argue over the details of the recipes.

But Julia wouldn't budge. Every recipe had to be tested. Every recipe had to be written clearly with the exact ingredients listed.

Julia wrote many versions of the cookbook. For nearly ten years she worked to perfect the 524 recipes that were included in the final draft. She believed that people were ready to learn how to cook better-quality food at home. Finally, an American publisher agreed to print *Mastering the Art of French Cooking*.

Julia had worked so hard on the book, she almost couldn't tell if it had all been worth it!

Her friend Avis answered the question for her. After spending years making test recipes from Julia's book, Avis wrote, "Honest to God, Julia, you have brought a revolution into this household. I wholly expect the completed book to cause a real revolution."

Little did Avis, Julia, or anyone else know that that's exactly what would happen.

Chapter 7
TV Star

When *Mastering the Art of French Cooking* was published in the fall of 1961, Julia took all the energy and dedication she had for writing the book and put it to use trying to sell it.

Julia and Paul were getting older. He was nearly sixty now, and she was almost fifty. Paul retired, and they decided to return to the United States. They bought an old house on a nice street near Harvard University in Cambridge, Massachusetts.

In Cambridge, Paul went to work making Julia's kitchen perfect. He built high counters so Julia wouldn't have to stoop. He put little hooks on the wall and hung all her shiny copper pots in neat rows. He made sure she had a big professional oven. There was plenty of space for Julia to mix, chop, knead, and dice.

Julia was standing in her new house with moving boxes still all around when a special delivery man brought a copy of *Mastering the Art of French Cooking* to her for the first time. It was big and heavy and so very pretty. It was cream colored, with little red-and-blue designs on the cover.

Book reviewers called it "glorious" and "brilliant" and "monumental." An important food writer for the *New York Times* even called it a "masterpiece."

Simca came to Cambridge to stay with Julia and Paul. The three of them traveled the country to promote the book. They talked to people about cooking French food.

They went to bookstores and big department stores. They even cooked right in front of shoppers. They wanted to demonstrate that even though French food was more complicated than American food, it was easy to cook if there were clear, simple instructions.

TV CHEFS BEFORE JULIA

ALTHOUGH SHE BECAME THE MOST WELL-KNOWN, JULIA CHILD WAS NOT THE *FIRST* TELEVISION CHEF.

IN 1946, JAMES BEARD STARRED IN THE FIRST NETWORK COOKING SHOW, *I LOVE TO EAT!* BEARD, WHO WAS KNOWN AS "THE DEAN OF AMERICAN COOKERY,"

JAMES BEARD

HAD WRITTEN MANY COOKBOOKS. BUT BEARD WAS NOT COMFORTABLE ON TELEVISION. HE DID NOT SMILE AND HE WAS NOT GOOD AT EXPLAINING HOW TO COOK. HIS SHOW LASTED ONLY ONE YEAR.

DIONE LUCAS HAD BEEN THE FIRST FEMALE GRADUATE OF LE CORDON BLEU. SHE WAS BRITISH, BUT SHE COOKED FRENCH FOOD AND TOOK IT VERY SERIOUSLY. HER FIRST COOKING SHOW, *TO THE QUEEN'S TASTE*, WAS SHOWN ON AMERICAN TELEVISION IN 1948. DIONE LUCAS WAS AN IMPORTANT INFLUENCE ON JULIA CHILD.

DIONE LUCAS

What really made Julia famous, though, was when she appeared on television to talk about French cooking.

Julia's television career started unexpectedly.

In February 1962, about four months after *Mastering the Art of French Cooking* was first available in bookstores, Julia was invited to appear on a Boston television program to talk about her book. When she arrived at the Channel 2 studio, though, she brought a frying pan, eggs, a spatula, and a hot plate—a small single burner to cook on.

No one in the TV studio that day knew what to do when Julia started to set up her tiny work station to make an omelet.

At six feet two inches, her height would not have mattered if she were sitting in a chair, as all the other guests did. But she was standing up at a counter, talking to the audience as she cracked, scrambled, and flipped the eggs.

This was a challenge for the cameramen.

Should they focus on Julia's hands or on her face? What if something went wrong and the eggs ended up on the floor? What if the host didn't like the eggs?

Julia made her omelet with the skill of a

professional chef. She spoke cheerfully about how simple it was. The show's host loved the omelet.

And the cameramen somehow figured out how to capture the cooking lesson, the very tall woman at the counter, and her happy personality.

By the next day, more than two dozen viewers had called and sent letters to the station, asking to see more of Julia. Everyone at Channel 2 realized immediately that she was something special.

Chapter 8
Branching Out

Even though they had never before considered adding a cooking show, Boston television executives were willing to give it a try. They called it *The French Chef.* The half-hour weekly show featured Julia cooking recipes from her book,

Mastering the Art of French Cooking. It debuted in February 1963 and was an instant hit.

In the first episode, Julia made a stew with beef, garlic, onions, mushrooms, and red wine.

In the second episode, she made French onion
soup, with a lot of onions, broth, wine, and
cheese. It was one of Julia's all-time favorite things
to eat.

In more than two hundred episodes over the course of ten years, Julia cooked for her adoring television audience. She stuffed sausages, boiled lobster, and even showed her viewers how to perfectly hard-boil an egg. She also made delicious desserts like chocolate cake and ice cream.

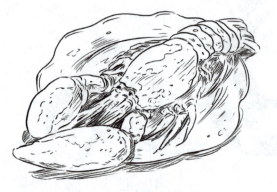

It wasn't always easy. Julia's show was recorded live. She had no chance to redo mistakes. If she made a mistake, she had to keep right on going with her recipe.

Once, Julia flipped a potato pancake into the air too enthusiastically. On its way down, it missed the pan and fell *splat* onto the table.

"You can always pick it up. If you're alone in the kitchen—who is going to see?" she sang into the camera as she plopped the pancake right back into the pan and kept cooking.

Her fans didn't mind one bit. In fact, they loved Julia even more for her mistakes, because they made mistakes in their kitchens, too. Julia took the stress out of cooking and made it seem fun.

"If I can do it, you can do it!" was her motto.

The French Chef started in Boston, but within
two years it was airing on nearly one hundred
television stations across the country. Julia was
a guest on other television cooking shows. She
became a regular on *Good Morning America*.

And no matter where she appeared on TV, Julia always ended her performance with the words *bon appétit*! This

Bon Appétit,

Julia Child

was Julia's shortcut for saying, "I hope you have a hearty appetite and that you enjoy your meal."

Even though she was now famous, Julia didn't give up writing. She wrote a regular food column with recipes and cooking advice for *The Boston Globe*. She also wrote more books. And in 1970, she and Simca published a second volume of *Mastering the Art of French Cooking*.

No matter how famous she became, Julia always had time for her fans. She spoke to them at book signings. She gave advice to young chefs. Julia even refused to get a private phone number. On Thanksgiving, strangers would call her in a panic.

They had questions about the right way to cook their turkeys. Julia was never too busy to take their calls.

As the years passed, Julia wrote about twenty books and appeared on more than a dozen televisions shows and TV specials about cooking. Julia Child had become a star.

Chapter 9
Return to California

In 1987, Julia was as popular as ever. But she was slowing down. When she was younger, Julia could work all day and into the night. She wrote books and made television shows and still had enough energy to host dinner parties. Nearing her eightieth birthday, she struggled to keep her energy up.

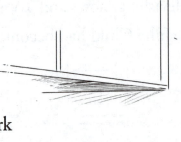

Her knees hurt and her doctors told her not to stand for long periods of time. During camera breaks, Julia would lean against the kitchen counter. Everyone could see she was in pain.

But when the cameras were turned on, Julia became her old self. She laughed, she cooked, and she spoke to her audience.

Julia still loved cooking and sharing her passion for food. She had a staff of assistants. Her kitchen at home had been turned into a TV set. She had always filmed the show right in her own home. As long as Julia kept working, she felt young.

This wasn't the case with Paul. He was ten years older than Julia. He had suffered a stroke.

It became very difficult for him to travel. By this time Julia and Paul had stopped visiting the small vacation home they had built together in France.

Paul had always been Julia's biggest helper during the filming of her television shows. He helped build her TV kitchen and coached her for her performances. Now, Paul often interrupted the filming. He stormed out of the kitchen. He seemed to be getting more confused. In 1994, at the age of ninety-two, Paul died.

Julia kept working. She wasn't ready to retire. In 1996, she starred in thirty-nine episodes of a new show called *Baking with Julia*. And in 1999, she co-starred with her friend, the famous French chef Jacques Pépin, in *Julia and Jacques Cooking at Home.*

JACQUES PÉPIN

JACQUES PÉPIN WAS BORN IN FRANCE IN 1935. HIS PARENTS OWNED A RESTAURANT WHERE JACQUES LEARNED TO COOK AND WHERE HE DEVELOPED HIS LIFELONG LOVE OF FOOD. IN HIS TWENTIES, HE MOVED TO PARIS TO BECOME A CHEF. AND IN 1959, HE MOVED TO THE UNITED STATES TO BEGIN WORKING IN AMERICAN RESTAURANTS.

TODAY HE IS A WORLD-FAMOUS CHEF, TELEVISION PERSONALITY, AND COOKBOOK AUTHOR WHO IS ALSO A DEAN AT THE INTERNATIONAL CULINARY CENTER, A COOKING SCHOOL IN NEW YORK CITY.

In 2003, Julia was the first woman inducted
into the Culinary Institute of America's Hall of
Fame. President George W. Bush awarded her a
US Presidential Medal of Freedom. And she even
received the French Legion of Honor—the highest
award given out in France—for making French
cooking popular in America.

By the time Julia turned ninety in 2002, she was in a wheelchair for much of the time and no longer appeared on television. She decided it was time to go home to California. It had been almost sixty years since she had left. Julia gave her house in Massachusetts to Smith College and moved into a retirement community in Santa Barbara, California.

But Julia still didn't retire. Paul's grandnephew, Alex, was a writer. He wanted to help her write one final book. It would be about Julia's time in France. She loved telling stories to Alex about her favorite times with Paul and the meals they shared.

In 2004, Julia's health worsened. But that didn't mean she had lost her appetite. One night in August, Julia was craving one of her favorite dishes, French onion soup. Millions of people had watched Julia prepare the soup on television over the years. Now, alone in her kitchen, Julia cooked a pot just for herself. It would be her last meal.

Julia Child died two days later on August 13. The *New York Times* called her "the French Chef for a Jell-O Nation." And Julia's legacy lived on.

In 2006, that final book, *My Life in France*, became a bestseller. And in 2009, the Oscar-winning actress Meryl Streep portrayed Julia in the movie *Julie and Julia*. The movie told the story of how a young woman named  Julie tried to cook all of Julia's recipes in one year. *Mastering the Art of French Cooking* even rose to the number one spot on the *New York Times* bestseller list—forty-eight years after it was first published. It seemed that Julia was as popular as ever.

In her will, Julia gave the contents of her
kitchen to the Smithsonian Institution's Museum
of American History. All the items were brought
to a gallery in Washington, DC, that was rebuilt
to look just the way Julia had left her kitchen.

WHAT'S IN JULIA'S JUNK DRAWER?

EVEN THE WORLD'S MOST FAMOUS TV CHEF HAD A KITCHEN JUNK DRAWER FILLED WITH ALL THE THINGS THAT DIDN'T QUITE BELONG ANYWHERE ELSE.

TODAY, YOU CAN SEE JULIA'S JUNK DRAWER AT THE SMITHSONIAN INSTITUTE IN WASHINGTON, DC. IT CONTAINS BITS OF STRING, RUBBER BANDS, DEAD BATTERIES, AND A CHAMPAGNE STOPPER GIVEN TO HER BY HER FRIEND AND FELLOW CHEF JAMES BEARD. IT ALSO HOLDS A SMALL COMB, A MIRROR, AND LIPSTICK, SO THAT JULIA COULD DO HER MAKEUP BEFORE HER DINNER GUESTS ARRIVED.

JULIA ALSO KEPT A SECOND MIRROR FROM HER WORLD WAR II DAYS IN THE DRAWER. IT'S AN OSS STAFF-SIGNAL MIRROR, USED TO SIGNAL PLANES OR HELP FIND LOST SOLDIERS. JULIA HAD KEPT THE MIRROR SINCE HER DAYS IN CHINA DURING WORLD WAR II.

Every year millions of people visit Julia's kitchen—one of the museum's most popular exhibits.

They see the special maple countertops custom made for Julia. They gaze at the copper pots hanging on the wall. They marvel at an oven that can fit two twenty-five-pound turkeys. Visitors can even hear Julia's recorded voice saying, "Keep to the kitchen and make it a real family room and part of your life." Standing there, with your eyes closed, you can almost see Julia raising her wine glass and adding, *"Bon appétit!"*

TIMELINE OF
JULIA CHILD'S LIFE

1912 — Julia McWilliams is born on August 15 in Pasadena, California

1934 — Graduates from Smith College with degree in history

1942 — Joins the Office of Strategic Services

1944 — Meets Paul Child in Ceylon, now Sri Lanka, where he is also stationed

1946 — Marries Paul Child in Pennsylvania

1948 — Moves with Paul from Washington, DC, to Paris

1949 — Enrolls at Le Cordon Bleu, the world's most famous cooking school

1951 — Starts a cooking school for American housewives with French cooks Simone (Simca) Beck and Louisette Bertholle. Starts work on a cookbook with them.

1961 — Moves to Cambridge, Massachusetts
Mastering the Art of French Cooking is published

1963 — *The French Chef* premieres on WGBH, Channel 2, Boston

1966 — *The French Chef* wins the first Emmy Award for an educational program

1981 — Julia launches The American Institute of Wine & Food

1989 — *The Way to Cook* is released

1994 — Paul dies at the age of ninety-two

2001 — Moves to a retirement home in California

2003 — President George W. Bush awards Julia the Presidential Medal of Freedom

2004 — Dies on August 13, 2004, at the age of ninety-one

TIMELINE OF
THE WORLD

Start of World War I — 1914

Alexander Fleming discovers penicillin — 1928

Stock market collapse marks start — 1929
of the Great Depression

Franklin D. Roosevelt elected president — 1932
of the United States

Attack on Pearl Harbor leads to the United States — 1941
joining World War II

End of World War II — 1945

The Soviet Union sends Sputnik into orbit — 1957

John F. Kennedy elected president — 1960
of the United States

The Beatles release their first album — 1963
Martin Luther King Jr. delivers
"I Have a Dream" speech

Neil Armstrong becomes the first man — 1969
to set foot on the moon

The Vietnam War ends — 1975

The first test-tube baby is born — 1978

The Berlin Wall falls, marking the reunification — 1989
of East and West Germany

Nelson Mandela is elected president of South Africa, — 1994
ending apartheid

Terrorists destroy the World Trade Center — 2001
in New York City

BIBLIOGRAPHY

Child, Julia, and Avis DeVoto. **As Always, Julia: The Letters of Julia Child & Avis DeVoto**. Edited by Joan Reardon. New York: Houghton Mifflin Harcourt, 2010.

Child, Julia, and Alex Prud'homme. **My Life in France**. New York: Knopf, 2006.

Collins, Kathleen. **Watching What We Eat: The Evolution of Television Cooking Shows**. New York: Continuum, 2009.

Conant, Jennet. **A Covert Affair: Julia Child and Paul Child in the OSS**. New York: Simon & Schuster, 2011.

Shapiro, Laura. **Julia Child**. New York: Viking, 2007.

Spitz, Bob. **Dearie: The Remarkable Life of Julia Child**. New York: Knopf, 2012.